Crescent Color Guide to
CATS

Jan,

For a girl I love
very much. Please
share this book with
Phred.

Love,
Ed
9/19/81

Crescent Color Guide to
CATS

Angela Sayer

Crescent Books
New York

Photography by Angela Sayer
(Tony Stone Associates: back cover, endpaper,
title spread, contents spread and pages 7, 13, 19,
37, 43, 75 left, 79. Bruce Coleman Ltd—Hans Reinhard·
front cover)

Copyright © The Hamlyn Publishing Group Limited
MCMLXXX

First English edition published by
The Hamlyn Publishing Group Limited
London · New York · Sydney · Toronto
Astronaut House, Feltham, Middlesex, England

Library of Congress Catalog Card Number: 80-65950
ISBN 0-517-31851-2

This edition is published by Crescent Books,
a division of Crown Publishers, Inc.
a b c d e f g h

Phototypeset by Tradespools Limited, Frome, Somerset
Printed by Litografía A. Romero, S. A.
Santa Cruz de Tenerife, Canary Islands (Spain)
D. L. TF. 349 – 1980

Contents

Introducing Cats

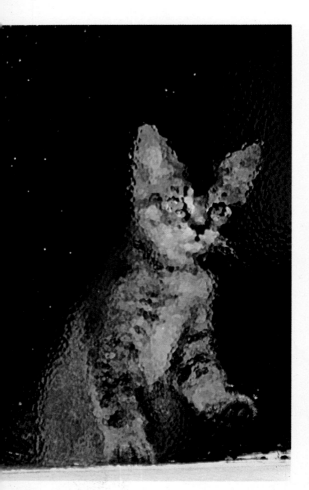

Even today, after centuries of living as a domesticated pet, the cat has retained the same mystique and aura of independence for which it was revered in the days of the Pharaohs.

All kittens are cute and appealing whether pedigreed or pet type, and all need the same basic essentials in life – good food, a warm bed and lots of tender, loving care.

For centuries the cat has played a major role in the lives of humans and has had a violent and eventful history, having been both worshipped as a god and persecuted as a devil. Now it has reached a position midway between the adulation heaped upon it by the peoples of Ancient Egypt and the terrible tortures meted out to it in the Middle Ages. Even today, too much cosseting can prove detrimental to the health of pet cats, and still some forms of cruelty must be guarded against. Although the first cats were probably domesticated by cavemen, who, for reasons best known to themselves, decided to allow cats to live with them instead of eating them, the first real records of cat-keeping date back to Egypt, about four thousand years ago. By this time, the cat had evolved successfully, having shared a common ancestor with dogs, bears, civets and other mammals: a tiny, tenacious, weasel-like creature called *Miacis*. This small mammal lived some 50 million years ago in the Eocene period, when the earth was undergoing violent changes, and only the forms of life most capable of adaptation could adjust sufficiently to survive and breed.

Over a time scale of many thousands of years, little *Miacis* evolved and prospered, and produced *Dinictis*, one of its descendants which first appeared in the Oligocene period about 30 million years ago. *Dinictis* went on to sub-divide into many subspecies during the following 10 million years, until in the Miocene era there were some ninety-five species, all directly related to our cats of today, and of which some forty species exist now in very similar and easily recognizable forms. Even the earliest cats were built for survival; small, neat and perfect carnivores. The evolution of the retractile claw was a masterpiece, for it allowed extra speed in the chase, with the claws sheathed. Then during the spring or pounce, these deadly weapons could be instantly exposed to grip the unfortunate victim. The cat's dentition too evolved perfectly, and provided two types of teeth, some to hold, stab and kill, and others to slice, biting the prey into pieces small enough to swallow easily.

In the days of the Pharaohs in Egypt, the cat was already well established as a friend and ally of man, proving its worth by killing rats and mice in the great grain stores of the time, and destroying the often poisonous snakes which sometimes slid into Egyptian homes. From the mummified remains of the period, two main types of cat have been identified; a large, heavy form of the Jungle Cat *Felis chaus*, which was probably used in the granaries and for wild-fowling, plus another neater species, *Felis libyca*, the African Wild Cat or Kaffir. For two thousand years a cult existed in Egypt during which time the cat in all its forms, domesticated or wild, was treated with reverence. The death penalty was enforced on anyone proved to have killed one of the sacred animals, and when a pet cat died, the whole family went into a period of full mourning, shaving off their eyebrows as a mark of respect, wailing, burning candles and beating gongs. Depending on the wealth of the dead cat's owner, it would be embalmed and enshrined, either in a simple papier mâché case or in a specially-made casket. Some were made from plain wood, others were jewel-encrusted, and made of gold or silver. The bodies of cats belonging to poor people were merely wrapped in layers of linen cloth, and paper circles were painted to represent the eyes. In Bubastis a great temple of red granite was erected, and dedicated to the glory of the cat-goddess Bast or Pasht, from whose name the word 'Puss' is thought to have been derived. Many cat mummies were discovered within the temple grounds and many thousands more discovered in cat cemeteries situated along the banks of the Nile.

The Ancient Egyptian word for cat is *mau* which also means 'to see', while a favourite amulet of the time was an *utchat* or 'sacred eye', often having many tiny cat figures engraved around a central, stylized eye. As *mau* closely approximates the natural sound of the cat, its close association with spiritual and magical matters is quite apparent. Cat amulets were fashioned of every conceivable material, and many still exist in museums and collections. Cats were often the subject of illustrations, and were shown in many different contexts. One famous painting shows a cat being used to catch water fowl, while another depicts the Sacred Solar Cat striking off the head of the serpent Apep, God of Darkness. At the time of the cat's veneration in Egypt, similar types of cat were known to have existed in China and India, though in a semi-wild state. The Egyptians were loath to part with their animals, but Roman soldiers did manage to smuggle a few specimens, and these were valued as vermin catchers. Later, wherever the Roman armies tramped, their precious cats went too, for the Romans were greatly influenced by the cults of the Egyptians.

As the paths of the great armies traversed the world, so the cat gradually spread, mating with the wild stock, producing kittens, and gradually becoming more and more tame. The Romans' fondness for their cats is shown by the number of camps that were named after them, such as Cat Vicense, now called Kattewyk, meaning Cats' Town. King Fergus I took the first Egyptian-type cat to Scotland, and wherever cats appeared they quickly established themselves in the service of man. So much so in fact, that special laws were introduced for their protection. Perhaps the most famous piece of legislation to be recorded was that innovated by Hywel Dda, King of Wales, in A.D. 936. He fixed severe penalties for killing cats, and his laws on the worth of a cat and her *tiethi* (qualities) were carefully enforced. The ruling classes of Europe, including Britain, counted cats among their prized possessions.

Cats were spreading far and wide, and those transporting them were inclined to select the more unusual colours and patterns whenever these could be found. The Crusaders brought back from the East some truly beautiful longhaired cats, the like of which had never been seen, and these then mated with the local shorthaired stock. The returning armies also unwittingly brought back the plague, and the value of cats was greatly enhanced by their usefulness in killing some of the rats carrying that dread disease. Despite their work, the Black Death overran Europe. Cats, by then in several shapes and colours, soon found comfortable niches catching vermin on farms, and in the city warehouses. They played an important role aboard ship and as perfect household pets.

Two very new breeds are pictured here. The Cameo Persian (above) was produced by mixing red and silver genes, which created several colour varieties. The Chocolate Colourpoint or Himalayan (right) was the result of a natural progression within the breed. This fine queen is *Champion Huntley Havoc*.

Fritz, the ginger tom cat, has lovely lustrous eyes. The fathomless depths of his pupils remind us of the old belief that the eyes of the cat were the mirrors of the human soul.

The Law of Hywel Dda — King of South Wales A.D. 936

The worth of a cat and her tiethi is this —
The worth of a Kitten from the night it is kittened
until it shall open its eyes is one legal penny.
And from that time until it shall kill mice,
two legal pence.
And after it shall kill mice, four legal pence,
and so it shall always remain.
Her tiethi are to see, to hear, to kill mice,
to have her claws entire, to rear and not to devore
her kittens and if she be bought and be deficient in any
one of these tiethi let one-third of her worth be
returned.
The worth of a cat that is killed or stolen is
determined thus: let its head be put downwards upon a
clean and even floor with its tail lifted upwards, and
thus suspended whilst wheat is poured about it until
the tip of its tail be covered — and that is to be its worth.
The worth of a common cat is four legal pence.
Whoever that sell a cat is to answer for her not going a
caterwauling every moon, and that she shall devore not
her kittens, and that she shall have ears, teeth and nails
and being a good mouser.

During the Middle Ages the cat's fortunes underwent a dramatic change, for a cult had arisen in the Rhinelands in which cats played a major role. Certain rites were held associated with Freya, the goddess of fertility, whose chariot was traditionally drawn by grey cats. The Church, thinking itself undermined by the ceremonies, initiated witch hunts. Legalized by the Pope, the persecution of witches began, and even to own a cat was to risk arrest, trial and torture. Unspeakable acts were committed and many thousands of innocent people suffered torment and martyrdom, their cats usually receiving the same punishments. The witch hunts spread across Europe, into Britain and later even to the Americas. Eventually, reason returned, and the resilient cat soon found its way back into the hearts and homes of people from all walks of life.

Today the cat is one of the most popular of all pets, especially for those people who live in apartments without gardens, for felines readily adapt to lives of total confinement when necessary. Their clean habits make the provision of toilet facilities relatively simple, and cats get all the exercise they need or desire running around indoors. Some people seem to think it cruel to confine a cat, but in these days of fast-moving traffic, and catnappers on the lookout for fun furs, Puss is better off at home. Pet cats should be neutered when approaching maturity, to prevent unwanted kittens and constant 'calling' in the female, and to avoid the noxious smell and antisocial behaviour of the entire tom. Properly fed, regularly groomed, and with a yearly check-up by the veterinary surgeon, the neutered cat makes a loving, perfect pet.

Bi-colour *Champion Midsummer Raffles* (right) and Blue Smoke *Mr Samson Jul* (far right) should both have deep orange or copper eyes.

The standard for the Brown Tabby in the United States allows only copper eyes, while in Britain the eyecolour may be copper, or hazel as seen in this magnificent male, *Oxus Mountain Ringlet* (below right).

In the pedigree breeds of cat, each variety has its own specific standard of points, giving its accepted eye colour. All the Himalayan patterned varieties have blue eyes of varying intensity, to correspond with the colour of their points. The Blue Colourpoint (above), *Champion Merryn Softus*, demonstrates true blue eyes.

Persian cats are typified by their massive build and luxurious coats. A fairly recent red variety is the flame-pointed Himalayan, showing identical type to a very old red breed, the Tortie, represented below by *Champion Wynmoor Diorama*.

To most people a cat is just a cat, and even the most ardent cat lover may be surprised to discover just how many cat breeds are to be found around the world, all officially recognized for show purposes. Pedigree cats come in two distinct types. They are defined by general conformation and bone structure. The first type is basically short and stocky, quite powerful in appearance and with strong bone. Its head is large and round, its body, neck and legs are short, its ears are small and its eyes are large and round. The second type is lighter, long and lithe with a longer, narrow head, large flared ears and almond-shaped eyes. The first group can be sub-divided also, according to hair length, and those which possess long, flowing coats are known as Persian or Longhaired breeds, while those with short hair are known variously as British Shorthair, American Shorthair or European Shorthair, depending upon their country of origin.

The second group contains all the Siamese, and the breeds derived from them, known as Foreign or Oriental Shorthairs, plus the unique breeds like the Abyssinian and Burmese, and we shall explore these in depth.

Right: Non-pedigree cats may be longhaired or shorthaired. They usually have generalized bone structure with no extremes of type.

Persian
or Longhaired Cats

Today's Persians are the descendants of two quite distinct types of longhaired cats which started to arrive in Europe in the sixteenth century. The first was the Angora, with its long silky coat, large ears and rather pointed face, and the second was the true Persian, massively built and thickly furred. The Angora came from Ankara in Turkey, and the Persian from Iran. Most of the Angora cats were pure white in colour, while the Persian variety tended to be black or a dark slate-blue. Quite indiscriminate interbreeding was carried out between the two types, and eventually the heavier Persian conformation superseded that of the lighter framed Angora. By the end of the eighteenth century owners of unusual cats began to take an interest in planned breeding, and started to record the pedigrees of their animals. People interested in the same varieties formed groups, and the very first cat shows were held in Britain and in the United States. The first official cat show was arranged by famous naturalist and artist, Harrison Weir. It was staged at the Crystal Palace in London in 1871 and proved to be a resounding success, providing a foundation stone for formation of today's flourishing Cat Fancy. Scotland's first cat show was held in Edinburgh in 1875, and in 1895, an Englishman visiting the United States organized America's first official cat show in New York City's Madison Square Gardens. Nearly two hundred cats competed and thus the American Cat Fancy was born. Clubs and Societies in both Britain and the United States flourished, the prize cat had arrived.

Omicron Ophelia **is a new and rare colour in Persian cats known as the Chocolate Tortoiseshell.**

Persian cats are delightful to own, each variety having slightly different characteristics, which make it the perfect pet for some particular household. These cats must be groomed daily however, and it is essential that anyone contemplating the purchase of a pedigree Persian kitten is prepared to undertake these regular brushing and combing sessions. The coat of the Persian is very long and flowing, and the undercoat is extremely soft. If grooming is neglected, the soft hairs are inclined to stick together and very soon form the hard knots and tangles known as mats. Once the Persian coat becomes matted, the only remedy is to cut out the matted hair with a pair of blunt scissors. When the tangles are cut away, the coat looks very patchy and unkempt, and naturally a clipped cat would stand little chance of winning on the show bench. Pet Persians are often clipped out under the belly during the summer months, especially in areas which achieve really high temperatures. But all in all, it is better to institute a proper grooming routine from the time the kitten is quite young, and to carry it out at the same time each day.

The equipment is quite simple, and consists of a bristle brush with a narrow head and three combs, one with wide teeth for the preliminary comb-through, one a little finer for removing small tangles, plus a fine-toothed comb for combing the face and checking for parasites. A pair of proper nail clippers is useful for trimming back the points of the claws if they grow too sharp. The grooming basket or box should also include some talcum or grooming powder, perhaps a proprietary grooming spray, and some cotton balls and buds. The cat is brushed all over, powder is rubbed into the coat if necessary to remove any grease or dirt, then, after allowing a little time for it to be effective, is brushed out. First the coarse comb is used, then the finer one. Cotton balls or buds are used to clean the corners of the eyes and in the ear flaps, and if the cat is one of the glossy colours such as black or tortoiseshell, a final spray of grooming lotion may be applied. During grooming, the cat should sit comfortably and the whole routine should be made as pleasant as possible, using especial care when dealing with tender areas under the body.

Persian cats today are all very similar, despite the diversity of colour and pattern available. Governing bodies of each country have official standards of points of perfection for each breed, and these are published so that breeders, exhibitors and also purchasers can find out just how each pedigree cat should look. The general standard for all longhaired cats is the same. The Persian should have a broad, round head with small, tufted ears set really wide apart. The face with its full, round cheeks, should have a short, broad nose and very large and expressive round eyes. The body must be stocky and the legs short and strong. The tail is often called the 'brush', being so full and bushy, and the long soft hair which frames the head is called a 'ruff'. These attributes make up a show Persian, whereas a pet Persian may acceptably fail in one or two points.

Cats with fur of just one plain colour are known collectively as Self-Coloured Longhairs in Britain, and as Solid-Colored Persians in the United States. In this division there are five old established colours, the Black, Blue, Red, White and Cream Persians, plus two recent additions, the exotic Self Chocolate and Self Lilac Longhairs, all with similar conformation. Longhaired cats, as we have said, come in many colours, and some of them are known by their coat colour which gives them their breed title. For example, the plain black longhaired cat is known as the BLACK PERSIAN or LONGHAIRED BLACK. Black Persians should have raven black coats, although kittens often have a slightly 'rusty' appearance when young. The eyecolour is deep orange or copper and any trace of green is considered to be a fault.

WHITE PERSIANS are sub-divided into three varieties according to their variable eyecolour which may be blue, when they are known as Blue-Eyed Whites; orange, giving us the Orange-Eyed Whites; or when one eye is blue and one eye is orange, when they are called Odd-Eyed Whites. In the United States, the orange eyecolour has been selectively bred for an increased depth of colour, so producing Copper-Eyed White Persians. Apart from the eyecolour, the standards for these white longhairs are the same, and all are equally attractive if kept in good condition.

The Self- or Solid-Colored Lilac Longhaired cat is another fairly new variety. This kitten, *Omicron Organdie*, has very good eyecolour for her age.

The Blue Persian standard calls for the eyes to be a deep orange or copper colour.

Today's BLUE PERSIAN is the most popular of the longhaired breeds, but when they were first exhibited they did not have a show class of their own and had to compete in the 'Any Other Variety' section. Many blue cats of those days had white markings, but eventually pure blue strains were isolated, and by 1901 the Blue Persian Club was formed to promote the breed. Strict standards were drawn up to encourage the members to aim for perfection in type and eyecolour, and the breed variety flourished. Queens and Princesses became besotted by the Blue Persians, and the breed became fashionable in society homes of Britain during Victorian times. Breeding stock was exported to many other countries of the world where type remains constant to the present day. The Blue Persian may be of any shade of blue, though judges do seem to prefer the paler tones. The coat must not show any signs of tabby markings or odd white hairs. In conformation, the show cat should be the same as any other Persian, large and cobby, but not coarse. Perhaps the most beautiful feature of all is the incredible eyecolour which is a very deep orange or copper complementing the subtle blue of the fur.

In the formation of the two new varieties, the chocolate gene was introduced, merely a modification of the black colouring in cats. SELF CHOCOLATE LONGHAIRS are the colour of milk chocolate, but otherwise conform to the general Persian Standard. The breed was developed experimentally in Britain in the 1970s and soon proved very popular. When Chocolate cats were mated with pure Blue Persians, black kittens were produced, but these carried the blue and chocolate genes, which, in combination enabled the cats to bear lilac coloured kittens when mated. The SELF LILAC LONGHAIRS are very beautiful, with a delicately tinted coat of palest lavender-grey, highlighted with lustrous orange eyes. Both Chocolate and Lilac Longhairs appeared in the same litters, and breeders were able to work on both varieties along parallel programmes.

Young kittens are
often found to have
very pale or
indeterminate
eyecolour at first.

The Cream Persian, showing his typical profile and magnificent full ruff (far right), is *Saharam Carcavelos*.

The RED PERSIAN is one of the rarest of the Self or Solid longhaired varieties, mainly because it is so difficult to breed without showing some tabby markings in the richly-coloured fur. Once known as Orange rather than Red, the early breeders tended to select the deepest, and therefore the most unusual, kittens in the litter as further breeding stock, and so over the years the colour deepened to the incredible rufous shade seen in the magnificent cats on the show benches of today. When a really good Self Red Persian is present at a cat show, it often generates great interest from the public and may well take top awards.

When CREAM PERSIAN kittens first appeared in litters they were thought of as 'sports' to be rejected, but eventually breeders realized that they were generated by the mating of a blue cat, to a red one. The blue gene is a simple diluting factor, and therefore when combined with red, merely diluted the red colour to cream. At first the Creams were known as Fawn cats, and indeed they are a very pale, warm fawn colour. The official breed standard asks for the coat to be of a pale to medium shade of cream, and if too gingery, it is termed 'hot'. Eyecolour in the Cream Longhair is particularly good and is of a deep copper shade.

The red factor is sex-linked in cats, and when red or cream cats are mated with those of the other solid colours, the beautiful range of Tortoiseshell coats may be produced. Tortoiseshells are almost always female, any males born are normally sterile, due to a genetic mistake. Those with red and black markings are known as TORTOISESHELL and the colours should be brightly patched. Cats with intermingled coats of blue and cream are called BLUE-CREAM PERSIANS and present an almost misty appearance. Recently, the red factor has been introduced into the chocolate and lilac longhaired varieties and the most attractive offspring are known as the CHOCOLATE TORTIE and LILAC CREAM LONGHAIR, respectively. The desired eyecolour of the tortoiseshell range of longhaired cats is similar, and may range from orange through to copper.

Britain's official standard for the Blue-Cream Persian insists on the blue and cream hairs being softly intermingled, and cats are faulted if the colours form patches in the coat. Conversely, the American cats are required to be patched, the blue predominating and the cream areas to be clearly defined. Whereas a solid coloured paw would be a bad fault in a British show, a Blue-Cream in an American show should have at least three paws of solid cream colour. Because there are no males in the tortoiseshell series of cats, the queens are usually bred to males with a coat colour to match one of those of the queen's coat. The resulting litters are often quite exciting with a whole range of coloured kittens present. For example, a Tortoiseshell female mated to a pure Black Persian male has Self Red and Black male kittens, while the female may be either Black or Tortoiseshell. A Blue-Cream female mated to a pure Blue stud cat, will have Blue and Cream male kittens while the females will be either Blue or Blue-Cream. However, if she is mated to a Cream male, the male offspring will still be Blue or Cream, but the females may be either Blue-Cream or Cream. Because of its sex-linked character, the red factor must be present in both of the parents before red or cream female kittens can be born.

It is difficult to breed top quality Red Self and Cream Persians without any barring or shadow markings on their coats. Here are two superb Persian Premier neuters; the Red is *Willowglen Tiger Tim* and his Cream companion is *Startops Honeybunch*.

Other Longhaired Cats

When the Himalayan factor was introduced to the longhaired breed some years ago, purist cat fanciers viewed the results with some misgivings. However, the dedicated work carried out over successive generations eventually produced an attractive and very popular breed known as the COLOURPOINT by the British, and the HIMALAYAN by the Americans. The breeding programmes were developed concurrently but quite separately on both sides of the Atlantic, but both breeds today have identical type. Of general Persian conformation, these cats are stockily built, with broad round heads topped by tiny ears. The coat is long and thick, and the tail is very well covered with long hair. Although they have the typical markings of a Siamese cat, which is caused by the presence of the Himalayan factor, in no way could this variety be called a longhaired Siamese or confused in any way with the Balinese cat. Rather, they are typical Persians with Siamese colouring. The gene restricting the basic coat colour to the points of the Himalayan has an associated gene which causes all Himalayan-patterned cats to have blue eyecolour. So whatever colour the points may be, the eyes will definitely be blue.

The colour range of the Colourpoint follows the normal Siamese pattern, and cats may be seen with Seal, Blue, Chocolate, Lilac, Red, Cream, Tortoiseshell, Blue-Cream, Chocolate-Cream or Lilac-Cream points. The Himalayans have the same colour range, but the Red-Pointed variety is known as the Flame-Point in the United States. At the present time some breeders have introduced the tabby gene into their Colour-point stock, and before long Tabby-Points, in all the accepted colours, will most probably be applying for official recognition by the governing bodies. Colourpoints and Himalayan cats make most delightful pets, and their unusual blue eyes make them particularly appealing. The variously coloured tortoiseshell-pointed females often have striking markings on their faces, and most breeders prefer a distinct red or cream blaze down the nose. No two faces are ever alike and the rather bizarre markings make the variety most attractive and highly sought after.

It is always better, if possible, to have two kittens which can grow up together. These Shaded Silvers will thrive in their new home and become inseparable, happy pets.

Champion Frallon Creampoint Apache is a Cream Colourpoint or Creampoint Himalayan, with very good type and beautiful blue eyes setting off the delicate colouring of his full coat.

Possibly the most beautiful of all the Longhaired cats is the exotic CHINCHILLA, which is basically white, with each long hair tipped with black giving the cat an overall sparkling appearance. The brick-red nose leather, and the lovely emerald or aquamarine eyes are also outlined in black, adding to this cat's theatrical look. It is a very photogenic breed and always in demand for commercial advertising films, and photographic modelling. The Chinchilla is one cat from a range known as the Silver Series. This is caused by the presence of a silver gene, which has the effect of removing pigment from the coat and leaving it white, or silver. In the Chinchilla, the greatest amount of black is removed and in some examples the cat has so little tipping that it does look pure white. In the intermediate example, the SHADED SILVER is produced, which is another beautiful animal in which the white hairs are heavily tipped with black, giving a shaded appearance. In the SMOKE LONGHAIR the coat is so heavily shaded that at first glance it may be mistaken for a black cat. As it moves, however, the silvery gleam of the undercoat shows through. When in full coat, the ruff is light and frames the face, and silver-white hairs fill the tiny ears.

The Smoke is often called the 'cat of contrasts', a very apt name, for the contrast between the ash-white undercoat and the black tipping is quite stark. Another dilute variety is officially recognized, called the BLUE SMOKE. It is identical to the Black Smoke except that where one is black, the other is a dark, definite blue. Due to the diluting effect of the blue factor, the contrast is less marked in this variety, so it is not quite as striking. Both Black and Blue Smoke cats have orange or copper eyecolour which adds to their pleasing expressions.

There is another silver longhaired cat, this time with the addition of the dominant tabby gene. The SILVER TABBY LONGHAIR has been around for at least one hundred years, but comparatively few are seen at today's shows. This is possibly because of the difficulty in breeding top-flight cats with the correct tabby pattern, along with accepted type and colour. This breed is very striking. The coat has a base colour of pale silver and the classic marbled tabby pattern is etched over this in black. The long coat diffuses the clarity of the pattern somewhat, but the correct distribution of the markings should be apparent. In the classic pattern, there should be a letter 'M' on the forehead, forming frownlines, and an unbroken line should run back from the corner of each eye. On the shoulders, the design should look like a butterfly with spread wings. A line runs from the butterfly configuration, along the spine to join the tail, with parallel stripes on either side. On each flank, oyster-shell shaped markings dominate, surrounded by more unbroken rings.

There are other colours in longhaired tabby patterned cats. Perhaps one of the oldest recorded pedigree cats, the BROWN TABBY LONGHAIR was certainly being shown at the end of the nineteenth century and seemed to have been a popular pet. It was at that time that cats were exported from Britain to the United States, and it is reported that a 'Brownie', newly arrived in his American home, was so desirable that an offer to buy him of one thousand dollars was made, but this was turned down by his proud new owner. At birth, Brown Tabby kittens are quite dark and their markings are very undecided. As the coat grows in, the markings gradually become more distinct, and it is an interesting fact that those kittens that have the heaviest, muddiest coat pattern while in the nest, generally develop into the best adults, with the correct black markings on a deep tawny basecoat. 'Brownies' are very dignified, self-assured cats, normally good tempered, and very independent. Affectionate and easy to maintain, they make ideal, kind, quiet and intelligent pets.

The RED TABBY LONGHAIR is also a very old-established breed, and may be easily distinguished from his non-pedigree counterpart, not only by his massive build, but by the very intensity of the rich red markings on his burnt orange coat. In the first cat shows, classes were for Self Red and Red Tabby combined, but eventually a clear distinction was drawn between the two varieties. It is just as difficult to breed a Red Tabby with the correct markings as it is to breed a Self Red without markings, but those who persevere are rewarded by top show awards. A really good specimen, with good markings and really deep colour is a very striking sight. And when he opens his huge eyes, they flash a deep copper-gold, practically matching the glowing shades of his coat.

The BLUE TABBY LONGHAIR is not recognized as a breed in Britain today, but in the United States it is possible to show them in the Persian group. Their ground colour is a blue-ivory and the classic pattern is in striking contrast, a very deep blue. Eyecolour should be copper.

A rare Blue Tabby Persian neutered female, *Oxus Holly Blue.*

When introduced to its new home, the Persian kitten will explore each new object and hiding place until its confidence grows, and it learns the whereabouts of its own bed or box.

When the red and silver genes are mixed together in the cat, the most interesting results are observed. The original crosses were made in the United States in 1954 and later in Britain, and the result has been the CAMEO series of longhaired cats. The palest of the Cameo cats is the fairy-like SHELL CAMEO, which has an ivory-white undercoat and a light tipping of red at the very ends of the hairs on the back, flanks, head and tail. The face and legs are lightly dusted with the red colour too, but the chin, stomach, chest and ear tufts are pure white. The overall effect is one of a delicately pink cat, the colour appearing a little unreal. In the darker SHADED CAMEO, the red tipping is increased and the cat appears to be wearing a red mantle over a white coat. It is a very striking, rare breed and has gloriously golden eyes. Darker still, due to even heavier tipping, is the RED SMOKE, which may even appear to be a Self Red cat until it moves and the stark white undercoat may be seen. With its dark red body and white ruff framing a red face, its red ears complete with white tufts, the Red Smoke is stunning.

A dilute form of Cameo is also bred. It is called the CREAM CAMEO and this is found in the Shell, Shaded and Smoke variations, just like its Red counterpart. The effect of cream with silver gives an even more ethereal effect, and it is often difficult to tell whether the kittens are normal Creams or Cameos. Tortie-Cream and Blue-Cream Cameo females are acceptable, and are very useful in breeding programmes. The Tortie-Cream has a white undercoat, overlain by tipping arranged in the normal tortoiseshell pattern of black, red and cream. Any intensity of tipping is acceptable for show purposes, but the cat should not have any solid areas of colour on its legs. The Blue-Cream Cameo is the dilute form of the Tortie, and is white with the tipped pattern in blue and cream softly intermingled. As in the standard cameo varieties, the accepted eyecolour is deep orange or copper. In the United States, the Shell Cameo is known as the RED CHINCHILLA, the Shaded Cameo as the RED SHADED, and the Red Smoke as the CAMEO SMOKE. Some associations also recognize CAMEO TABBY, which is a striking cat, white with a red tabby pattern.

Many of the standard Persian colours are bred with the addition of a gene which produces areas of white patches that conceal some of the body pigmentation. Some breeds exist as bi-coloured varieties, and some as tri-colours. When White is added to Tortoiseshell, the handsomely patched TORTIE-AND-WHITE LONGHAIR appears, called the CALICO in the United States. It is interesting to note that they were once known as Chintz cats in Britain. Like the Tortoiseshell, the Tortie-and-White is an all-female variety, but the addition of the white areas makes the black and red patches seem even brighter. The dilute form of Tortie-and-White is very attractive, with large patches of blue and cream interspersed with white. Often called the Blue-Tortie-and-White in Britain, its American name is much neater; DILUTE CALICO. Whether shown in Britain or the United States, the standards underwrite the fact that brindling (that means the presence of odd white hairs) is not permitted in the coloured areas. The American standards ask for a distinctive blaze of red or cream running down the face, and though not specified in the British standards, breeders and judges alike find a blaze very appealing.

Black-and-White cats known as Magpie Cats were shown at the turn of the century. The Magpie cat was black with white on the chest and feet. A white necklace of fur encircled the neck and the face was bisected by an even white blaze. Eventually the Magpie faded into obscurity, but today we have a thriving breed in the BI-COLOURED LONGHAIR, or in the United States, the BI-COLOR PERSIAN. Both of the bi-coloured breeds are restricted to black, blue, red or cream, all with white. The British standard states that not more than two-thirds of the cat's coat must be coloured; on the other hand not more than one-half of the coat must be white. The American standard calls for a blaze in the form of an inverted 'V'. The bi-coloured cats are very pretty, and the dilute colours are attractively set off by the white of the vest. They are calm and composed cats, taking life very much as it comes. The males are very useful for breeding with Tortie-and-White queens, and the symmetry of their patching is generally passed on to their offspring.

American Champion *Cotton Patches Holly*, a striking Calico queen.

Right: British Champion *Midsummer Raffles*, a Cream-and-White Bi-coloured male.

Unusual and Semi-Longhaired Cats

A Seal-Pointed Birman cat, sometimes called the Sacred Cat of Burma. One of the unique longhaired breeds with its origins steeped in legend.

One of the most popular of the semi-longhaired varieties is the handsome BIRMAN, or Sacred Cat of Burma. This cat possesses the Himalayan factor which causes it to have a pale body and darker points, like the Colourpoint and the Siamese; but in addition it has four striking white paws. On the forefeet, the white area is sharply defined and is cut off like a glove at the wrist, while on the hindfeet, the white areas come to points at the heels, and are referred to as 'gauntlets'.

A charming legend exists to explain the rare patterning of the Birman, and the story has followed the cat across the world from the temples of its birth, through France to Britain in 1960, and eventually to the United States. The legend tells how, many centuries ago, a temple was built in Asia by the Khmer people, in which to worship Tsun Kyan Kse, the sapphire-eyed goddess who presided over the transmutation of human souls. Mun Ha, High Priest of the Kittahs was very old, and spent long hours kneeling in contemplation before the great golden statue of the goddess. He was always accompanied by his oracle, a large, white longhaired cat called Sinh, who sat, unmoving, gazing at the deity with his steady gold-flecked stare. One evening as the moon rose behind the mountains, a horde of Siamese barbarians attacked the temple gates, and Mun Ha, as he prayed earnestly before the statue for the deliverance of the temple, suffered a heart attack and died, his face filled with anguish. Sinh, the cat, jumped quickly up to the sacred throne to guard his master's body, placing his paws protectively on Mun Ha's silvery head, and looking up for help, into the eyes of the goddess.

It was then that the miracle of transmutation took place. For as Sinh held this position, the glistening white hairs of his back changed to the light golden tone irradiated by the statue. And his yellow, golden-tinged eyes suddenly became the same sapphire-blue as those of the goddess. Sinh's nose, ears, tail and legs darkened until they matched the colour of the earth beneath the throne, all except for the paws, which still clutched his beloved master's head, and these remained purest white. As the transformation took place, the other frightened priests gathered round, but Sinh's impelling stare rallied their flagging spirits. They closed the temple gates and fiercely attacked and vanquished the invaders. Seven days passed then, sadly, Sinh the sacred cat also died, and through the power of the goddess carried the perfect soul of his master, Mun Ha, with him to Heaven.

Far right: Bright auburn markings on a clear white silky coat distinguish the rare Turkish Van or Swimming Cat.

Roselu's Aztec, a red tabby Maine Coon, peeks out of his carpeted playbox.

The MAINE COON is a breed native to the United States. It originated there over a hundred years ago in its home state of Maine. Early written records are somewhat sketchy, but legends and stories abound regarding the animal's roots. One very romantic legend, often retold, is that the prized cats of Queen Marie Antoinette were secretly shipped to America at the time of the French Revolution, to be hidden away until she could herself escape and rejoin them in safety and exile. Another theory put forward insisted that the cats were the result of crossmating between ordinary domestic cats and raccoons. The coat of the Coon is very similar to that of the Angora, the first longhaired cat known to have reached the New World; and crossed with the local domestic shorthairs, the offspring would have eventually and quite naturally produced longhaired kittens.

Free-roaming, tough and hardy, the Maine Coon has developed into a distinct type, its rugged coat evolving to suit the extremes of weather experienced in the area in which it developed. Visitors to Maine became captivated by the qualities of the local cats and often took kittens away with them, thus spreading the breed far and wide. The Coon was highly favoured for its hunting abilities, and proved to be an affectionate but undemanding housepet. Books written at the turn of the century record the existence of the Maine Coon, and one of the breed took Best in Show at the Madison Square Gardens Cat Show in New York City during 1895. With the increasing popularity of the exotic foreign imported cats, the Coon suffered a decline in the show ring, but by 1960 groups of Coon fanciers revived the breed.

Maine Coon cats have unique personalities. Their fans say that no two are alike. They use their paws a great deal, for scooping food and drink and playing with the water in their drinking bowls. Remaining active and playful all their lives, Coons make pleasing pets, and their coats, shortish over the shoulders and saddle, long and flowing on the side and underneath are easy to groom and resist matting. Perhaps best of all is the wide range of coat colours and patterns – one to suit any taste or fancy.

Many breeds have blue varieties, for blue is a simple genetic dilution of black. Above is an attractive Blue Birman kitten, *Hephziban Caerulus of Mask Rider*; below, a beguiling Blue Turkish Angora Premier and quadruple Champion *Gnirha's Amy of Derry Downs*.

A very ancient breed, the TURKISH ANGORA originated in Ankara, the capital of Turkey, which was known as Angora in ancient times. This city was renowned for its longhaired animals, notably Angora rabbits, several longcoated dog breeds, and the Angora goat from which mohair is obtained. Ankara today is a very animal-conscious city and has had a successful zoological park for many years, in which pure white Angora cats are kept. Careful breeding programmes are followed and very strict records have been kept for years. Although the zoo concentrates only on the white Angora, it was recorded in a letter dated 11 May 1856, addressed to the President of the French Zoological Society, that the writer had found many examples of the Angora breed during his travels in the East. The very finest belonged to the Archbishop of Van in the east of Kurdistan on the border with Azerbaijan. Only one was typically pure white, another was completely coated in soft pearl grey, while the third was auburn with black and white flecks. All three were of magnificent build and had wonderfully long, silky coats.

A century later, two English travellers discovered some cats very similar to the old Angora type. These were in the Van district of Turkey. The cats had pure white fur, with bright auburn markings on their faces and tails. On making further enquiries, the two ladies found that a whole race of them existed, and that the cats were greatly prized. All were privately owned and although basically shy, dignified cats, had a unique trait: a penchant for swimming, jumping quite voluntarily into the shallow rivers and warm pools of the area during the hot summer months. A pair of kittens was acquired and transported back to England, where, with further additions during future years, a true-breeding variety was established. Known as the Turkish Cat, as distinct from the Turkish Angora, the two breeds are similar in bone structure and the quality of the long, silky hair.

The Turkish was given official status in Britain in 1969. The Angora is accepted only in the United States.

Although they do have long hair, the three kittens here do not conform to any breed standard.

The Himalayan factor which produces the dark points of the Birman is also responsible for the markings on two other American breeds, the Balinese and the Ragdoll. The BALINESE arose as a spontaneous mutation in several litters of pure-bred Siamese cats during the early 1950s in the United States. All had typically long, svelte, Siamese-type bodies and developed the normal Siamese colouring on their points, but in addition, they had semi-longhaired coats of rather fluffy fur. At first, breeders disposed of them as pets, but eventually, the little oddities were mated together and proved to breed true, and a new breed was born. After studying their exciting new cats closely, and being totally captivated by their elegant lines and graceful, flowing movements, the original breeders were reminded of the exotic dancers of Bali, and decided to choose the evocative name Balinese. This was officially accepted by the Cat Fanciers' Association of America in 1970, since when the breed has gone from strength to strength. Happy, lively and very affectionate, the Balinese is a Siamese cat in every respect except for its coat, and has the usual Siamese points' colours of Seal, Blue, Chocolate and Lilac.

RAGDOLLS are totally unique and very large cuddly cats, flopping happily on their backs, curled in their owners' arms, just like big stuffed toys. Originating from a white cat called Josephine, the breed was created in the United States, where it is officially accepted by some of the registering bodies. All based on a Himalayan-patterned coat, the Ragdoll comes in three types, the Bi-color, the Mitted, or the Colorpoint, and all may have the basic Siamese or Himalayan colourings of Seal, Blue, Chocolate and Lilac, just like the Balinese. The Bi-color sports a white chest and blaze in addition to its dark points, while the Mitted variety has just pure white paws, and the Colorpoint has normal dark mask, legs and tail, just like the Colourpoint Persian. Fans of the breed say that they are so compliant that a sleeping Ragdoll may be picked up, carried around and put down without being awakened. Fighting between them is unheard of, and they have a high pain tolerance. Ragdoll males often reach 20 lb at maturity but are quiet, loving and docile. The queens make excellent mothers and the kittens are adorable.

A Sable Spotted Turkish Angora, *Sibir Pekeira*.

SOMALI is the exotic African name given to a North American breed which is merely the longhaired form of the normal Abyssinian. Some of the early Abyssinian cats are known to have carried longhair genes in their makeup, and as recessive genes can remain dormant for many years it was inevitable that sooner or later two Longhair 'carriers' would mate and produce offspring to surprise, and hopefully, delight their owners. After the initial shock of seeing fluffy kittens in otherwise normal litters, breeders realized the potential of developing them into a new variety. After they had worked consistently for eight years, and the Somali Cat Club of America had been formed in 1972, the breed was given championship status by the Cat Fanciers' Association of America. The Somali looks like a jungle cat, with its silky, rufous coat and long, full brushlike tail. Typically Abyssinian in head and body type, it is a long, lithe cat: hard, muscular and very active and alert. Its medium wedge head is topped by large, slightly pointed ears which are tufted at the tips and furnished with lots of hair inside. Large, bright almond-shaped eyes of deep gold or green, outlined with dark pigment, add to this cat's attractive appearance. The Somali is not bred in the United Kingdom, but is becoming increasingly popular in the United States and Canada where it is beginning to achieve high awards at shows.

In the Manx breed a similar occurrence took place when, despite the fact that shorthaired cats had been used for at least eight generations, the occasional longhaired kitten was produced. In Canada, these cats are called the CYMRIC, which is a Welsh word which just means 'Welsh', but in the United States the breed is known as the Manx Longhair. Apart from the length of coat, the Cymric is exactly like the normal Manx with a broad head and high cheekbones. The short neck and good shoulder balance the higher, rounded rump, and the short back adds to the powerful effect of the cat. There should be a little dimple at the coccyx where the tail would normally be, but sometimes a fringe of hair softens this effect. Virtually all recognized coat colours and patterns are found in this breed, just as in the ordinary Manx, along with their corresponding eye colours, and the long double coat is easy to maintain.

39

Shorthaired Cats

The Odd-Eyed syndrome is found in shorthaired as well as in longhaired cats. One eye is blue and the other eye generally yellow, gold or copper.

The cobby, stocky shorthaired varieties of pedigree cat bred to exacting standards are known in Britain as the British Shorthairs, in the United States as American Shorthairs, and in most European countries as European Shorthairs. With subtle variations in the desired bone structure, and the addition or subtraction of various colours and patterns here and there, the Shorthairs are a fairly homogeneous group. Like the Persians, they are basically given the names of their coat colour to denote their breed, and they are also grouped into Self- or Solid-Coloured, Non-Self or Non-Solid colours according to the country of their origin. Shorthaired cats are very undemanding as pets and totally independent. They can live happily in the normal family home and tolerate dogs, other cats and human babies equally well. Spotlessly clean in their habits, they really prefer to be out and about if possible, and do not do so well in cattery situations as their Oriental cousins. The short but thick coat is efficient in keeping out the cold, and so the shorthaired cats need less heat than the foreigns. They are very easy to groom, and merely need combing through once a week or so, to remove dead hairs and dust from the coat. The ears can be checked for accumulations of wax at the same time, and the claws checked to see if any are broken or over-long, needing to be trimmed back. Even for showing, very little extra grooming is required, and a bath of heated bran rubbed well into the hair, and thoroughly brushed out again some ten minutes later, cleans, freshens and revitalizes the entire coat.

Shorthaired queens generally have fairly small litters, averaging three kittens, but these are quite large at birth and grow on very rapidly. They eat at four weeks and can be weaned at six to seven weeks. The queens usually make excellent mothers, and take very good care of their babies. They lactate well, producing rich milk, but at weaning time encourage their kittens to eat solid foods.

The standard for the BRITISH SHORTHAIR calls for a hard muscular cat, the males being larger than the females. The head should be broad with full cheeks and a very firm, strong muzzle. The ears are medium in size, and it is important that they are set so far apart that the base of the inner ear is in a perpendicular plane with the outer corner of the eye. The neat ears are broad at their bases but have gently rounded tips. The eyes of the British Shorthairs are a really beautiful feature, being large, round and lustrous. Colour varies, of course, depending on the variety. The body of the Shorthair is quite large, with strong, flat shoulders, a broad rounded chest, and an overall impression of strength and power. The legs are quite sturdy but not coarse, and the paws are neat and rounded. The rather thick tail should be of a length to balance the body. The texture of the shorthaired coat is very important for showing and although it must be short and resilient to the touch, it must not be woolly or have an extra undercoat. The colours and patterns are clearly defined as we shall see later, and each colour and pattern of the Shorthair breed must have its corresponding eyecolour.

The AMERICAN SHORTHAIR has a very similar set of requirements: the main point in which the standards differ is in the length of the nose, which is short and broad in the British standard, and medium in length with a gentle curve in the American standard. The Cat Fanciers' Association of America also penalizes the Shorthair for having an extra short tail, for being overweight or too thin, having fluffy fur, or any indication of having been crossed with another breed.

One of the strangest mutations to occur among the shorthaired cats in America was the one which produced the AMERICAN WIREHAIR in the mid-

1970s. Its conformation is very similar to the normal-coated shorthaired varieties, but it is of a slightly lighter build. It is the amazing coat which distinguishes the breed from all others, for it is springy, dense and resilient, each hair coarse and wiry to the touch. The Wirehair can be found in a wide range of colours including White, Black, Blue, Red and Cream and several shades of Smoke and Tabby.

Another rare shorthaired variety is the CAMEO SHORTHAIR, not yet recognized in Britain, but accepted in the United States. It looks almost white in the Shell variety, but the hairs are just tipped with pale red giving it a characteristic, sparkling glow. There is also a Shaded variety in which the tipping is more intense and the cat looks far more red. Both varieties have brilliant golden eyes.

A shy and pensive, pale Shell Cameo Shorthair kitten.

The Cream Shorthair (above left) is a pale fawn in colour, while the Cameo Shorthair (above right) looks pale pink, due to the addition of silver hairs in the undercoat. Much brighter in colour is the Red Tabby Shorthair (centre) with dark red markings in a Classic pattern on a rich apricot base coat.

Far right: Mongrel cats are generally found in less striking colours and often have random white markings and socks like this sweet little pet kitten.

The Self-Coloured British Shorthairs are the Black, the Blue, the Cream and the White. The BRITISH BLACK is a truly magnificent cat, with great copper eyes gazing from an ebony face. There is no way in which it can be confused with the domestic black cat. BRITISH BLUE cats are by far the most popular of all the British Shorthairs, and are a simple dilute form of the Black. Also massively built, they have coats of a soft, even blue and particularly good type, accentuating the broad round head with its wonderful orange or copper eyes. BRITISH CREAM cats are a little less popular, being somewhat difficult to breed without ghost tabby markings showing through their pale creamy coats. A good specimen is very attractive, as the copper or orange eyecolour greatly enhances the warm tones of the coat.

The other self-coloured cats are the Whites, which are named according to their eyecolour, just as in the Persian group. There is the BLUE-EYED WHITE, the ORANGE-EYED WHITE, known as Copper-Eyed in the United States, and the ODD-EYED WHITE which has one eye each of orange and blue. The White Shorthairs are dainty cats and seem more graceful than their darker cousins, but this is probably only an optical illusion. The Blue-Eyed variety is sometimes found to be deaf which can be a great disadvantage to a cat. The Odd-Eyed cats result from matings between those with orange and blue eyecolour, and if an Odd-Eyed White inherits deafness from one parent, it is normally deaf only in the ear situated on the side of the head which has the blue eye. Blue-Eyed kittens are sometimes born with a dark smudge between their ears, which is said to indicate good hearing.

The Non-Self British Shorthairs form a large group including all the Tabbies, the Torties, the Bi-colours and the Smoke, as well as the recently recognized BRITISH TIPPED. This cat has a pure white coat lightly tipped on the ends of each hair with any accepted colour such as black, blue, red and so on. The black-tipped variety is very striking, looking like the shortcoated version of the Chinchilla, complete with boldly outlined eyes. The Silver is the only cat of this variety allowed to have green eyecolour. All other Tipped cats, according to the standard, must have eyes of copper or orange.

TORTOISESHELL cats are black with brilliantly patched areas of red and cream, and usually have a red or cream blaze bisecting the face. The colours seem brighter than in their longhaired equivalents as they are not diffused by so much hair. The dilute version of the Tortoiseshell is the BLUE-CREAM and here the colours must be softly intermingled, giving a shot-silk effect. No blaze is wanted in this variety, as solid patches of colour are considered faults. When the Tortoiseshell has large areas of white patching it is known as the TORTIE-AND-WHITE. Its colours must be evenly distributed, white must never predominate, and a small white blaze is highly desirable. BRITISH BI-COLOUR cats, like the Persians, may be of any acceptable cat colour, with white, and symmetrically marked ones are favoured.

Right: A Grand Champion, *Portrait's Romeow*, a fine example of a silver classic tabby American Shorthair.

In the beginning, all cats were tabby, for this is the natural colour of the wild cat, proven many times by genetic experiments which show that tabby, known as 'wild-type' is dominant to all the other colours in the domestic cat. The original tabby pattern was called *torquata* and was semi-striped with a great deal of agouti-like ticking in the ground coat. It is now thought that the first mutation to occur modified this wild-type to the pattern known as classic, marbled or blotched, and designated *catus*. Whatever the origins, we now have a series of tabby patterns, dominated by the ticked, as seen in the Abyssinian, then comes the mackerel-striped pattern which is thought to be closely linked, genetically, with the spotted pattern, then finally the classic design of marbled whorls. In the Shorthairs, the classic pattern is found in three varieties, the SILVER TABBY, the RED TABBY and the BROWN TABBY, and all these are seen at British cat shows, although the Brown is quite rare while the Silver is very popular. SILVER SPOTTED cats are also very popular, but although Brown and Red 'spotties' are also acceptable, very few are seen on the bench. The Tabby patterns show up really well on the short coats of the British breeds, especially the silvers, where the dramatic black pattern on silver makes a striking contrast.

Above: A litter of British Silver Tabby kittens, six weeks old and becoming very adventurous.

One other silver breed exists in the British Shorthair, and that is the SMOKE. Bred in Black and Blue varieties, both have pale silver undercoats, heavily tipped with either Black or Blue, producing a smoky, shaded effect. Any tabby markings are a fault in this breed, and so is incorrect eyecolour, only yellow or orange being allowed. A shorthaired breed unique to France is the large Blue cat known as the CHARTREUSE which is said to be descended from some Blue cats owned by the Carthusian monks in their monastery La Grande Chartreuse. First shown in 1931 in Paris, the breed declined sharply during the Second World War, and many important documents and records relating to the breed were lost. Outcrosses were made to help re-establish the big blue cat, and some good specimens were imported into the United States where work on the breed began in earnest during 1970. The Chartreuse has been identified both with the British and the Russian Blue, but is not like either, though it has some of the traits of both breeds. The typical specimen is a large cat with a head that is broad but not round. The nose is short with a slight stop in the profile and the face has a sweet, smiling expression. The small to medium ears are set high and have rounded tips, and the large expressive eyes may range from palest gold to a very deep orange.

The British Blue is a chunky cat with the perfect temperament for a housepet.

45

Although the pedigree shorthairs are recognized in a wide range of coat colours, the silvers are very popular.

The history of the American shorthair is more recent than that of shorthaired breeds of Britain and the rest of Europe, for there were no indigenous domestic cats in the North American continent. Immigrants over the years brought cats of many kinds, and carried them, along with their other possessions, in search of new lands. Eventually, pedigree shorthaired cats were imported from Britain at the turn of the century and an interest in breeding fancy cats began. The AMERICAN SHORTHAIR, when originally shown, competed in Housepet Classes, but were gradually bred selectively until the breed was standardized, with its own classes at shows. Very similar to the British Shorthair in build, the American is larger, and has a longer nose than its British counterpart. It has a very good temperament, and makes a delightful companion.

Not to be confused with the American Shorthair is the EXOTIC SHORTHAIR of the United States. This is a man-made breed produced by carefully planned matings between the best American Shorthaired cats and good examples of the Persian breeds. The aim was to develop a cat which combined the massive type of the exhibition Persian with a coat of medium length. The resulting breed is very popular as it is easy to maintain in good condition, requiring much less grooming than its long-haired cousins. The Exotic Shorthair is not recognized in Britain. The distinctive look of the Exotic is due to its extreme Persian type. The head is very round, with tiny ears set very wide apart and tilted slightly forward, adding to the round appearance of the head shape. The short, snub nose is quite broad and has a break in the profile. The cheeks are very full, the jaws broad and strong, and the chin is very pronounced and well developed. The massive head has incredible eyes, which being large and round, and set very wide apart, rather give the impression of a benevolent owl. The Exotic's body is thickset and cobby, low on the legs and with a deep chest. The hind end is equally strong and the whole cat looks well balanced and tough. The coat of the Exotic has a special texture, for although it is short to medium in length, it is also dense and plushy and springs up under the touch, its density causing it to stand away from the skin. This breed may be found in all the colours accepted in the American Shorthair group.

46

The ears of the Scottish Fold have a definite fold line. Those of *Denisla Morag* are very tightly folded forward.

The Fold is a large cat when adult and has a massive round head set on a short, thick neck, giving a strong and powerful appearance.

The SCOTTISH FOLD is the result of a natural mutation. It is a short-haired breed, very similar in conformation to the British and American Shorthairs, but is quite unique in having ears which fold forward and point down towards the eyes, instead of pricking up in the normal way. The first Fold was discovered in a Scottish farmyard in 1961. She was of unknown origin, pure white in colour, and as well as having such extraordinary ears, sported a very short, thickened tail. This little cat, Susie, eventually produced kittens with folded ears, one of which was acquired by a cat fancier who decided to try to develop the cats into a properly documented, acceptable breed. The young Fold male was mated to a British Shorthair queen which produced five kittens, all with tightly folded ears, and the breeding programme was under way.

Setbacks were encountered when it was discovered that when mated like-to-like other skeletal anomalies were produced, in addition to the folded ears, and after months of discussions, veterinary analyses and expert advice, the Governing Council of the Cat Fancy decided not to allow the Scottish Fold recognition or registration privileges. This effectively prevented the breed's exhibition at any official cat show and was a great blow to the Fold's enthusiastic admirers. The breeders decided to carry on with their plans however, and breeding stock was exported from Scotland to Europe and to the United States, where more liberal opinions as to the breed's viability were apparent. It was only when like-to-like matings were made that the problem of skeletally malformed kittens arose, so as the gene which produces the unusual ear is dominant, it was only necessary for one parent to be a Fold in order to get Fold kittens. Breeders mate their best Folds to really good examples of British or American Shorthairs, and expect to find half the resulting litter to have folded ears.

The Fold's ears accentuate the roundness of the head. Folds have lovely large, full eyes, the colour of which must be complementary to the coat colour. The short cobby body is powerful and strong, and the coat is short, but thick and dense, soft to the touch. The Scottish Fold has a tremendous personality and is a loving, gentle cat, good with children, living happily with other pets.

MANX cats owe their taillessness to a dominant mutant gene and when mated like-to-like, one in four of the resulting kittens is expected to die *in utero*. Manx may be mated quite successfully with Shorthair cats, and produce a ratio of tailless kittens, called 'Rumpies', some with short tails, called 'Stumpies', and some with normal, long tails. As its name implies, the Manx comes from the Isle of Man off the west coast of England, but it is unlikely that the curious cat mutated there. A ship of the Spanish Armada of 1588 was wrecked off the Manx coast, and it is believed that the ship's cats swam ashore at low tide. Many Eastern cats had stunted tails at that time, and some ship's cats are known to have been tailless. Marooned on the island, cats with the effective gene would soon pass it on to the local cat population. The Isle of Man has its own breeding cattery where it keeps several tailless cats, but although these are genuine Manx, they do not conform to the standards of the exhibition Manx seen at cat shows all over the world. Show Manx are similar to British and American Shorthairs in build, but they must have a high, rounded rump with a dimple at the coccyx where the tail would normally be rooted. The extra long back legs and lack of tail give the Manx a peculiar hopping gait rather like a rabbit, and it was once called the 'Bunny Cat'.

Champion Sunacres Rosey Dawn, a red tabby and white Manx queen.

Foreign Breeds

Top: *Taishun Abigail*, a normal or ruddy Abyssinian queen enjoying a hunt in the garden at dusk.

Heavily marked Abyssinian kittens like this five-week-old youngster, *Chezchats Steinway*, often develop the clearest and best ticked coats when they reach adulthood.

The various Foreign Shorthaired cats are totally different from the American and British Shorthairs, being basically longer, and lithe with slim bodies, legs and tails. Head shapes vary depending on the variety, but they are generally long and usually wedge-shaped, with large pricked ears and almond-shaped eyes. Foreign Shorthairs are very easy to keep, as they require the minimum of grooming, are very clean and affectionate, and most prefer their people to their homes. This last trait means that they travel well and make good companions. ABYSSINIAN cats are a unique breed, having coats which are ticked rather like those of wild rabbits. The colour is much more rufous however, and the ticking appears as two or three bands of dark colour towards the tip of each hair. Medium in size, the Abyssinian is an active, lively cat, interested in all that is going on around it and makes an excellent companion for anyone who is housebound or alone.

This breed is of modified Foreign type, having a pretty, heart-shaped face and large pointed ears. Some Abyssinian cats also have lovely ear-tufts which enhance their jungle look. The eyes in this cat are almond-shaped, large, brilliant and very expressive, and are subtly outlined with dark pigment. The American standard allows eyecolour to be either gold or green, while in Britain, Abyssinians may have eyes of amber, hazel or green. The normal or original colouring of this cat, known as the RUDDY ABYSSINIAN, is a rich golden-brown, ticked with various shades of brown or black, the undercoat is rich apricot in tone, and extends right down to the skin. The underside of the cat harmonizes with the apricot undercoat. The tail tip and the back of each hind leg up to the hock is black. The RED ABYSSINIAN, also known as the SORREL ABYSSINIAN, is a glorious, glowing deep apricot, ticked with chocolate-brown, while the BLUE ABYSSINIAN has steel-grey ticking on a warm, blue-grey base. An Abyssinian cat is faulted at shows for areas of white hair, a 'necklace' of dark hairs, or an abnormal tail.

At birth some Abyssinian kittens have very dark backs, dark marks on their stomachs and dark bars on the front legs. They often have a 'necklace' of dark hair ringing the neck too, and the inexperienced may look aghast at these apparent rejects. In fact, the heavily marked kittens may well turn out as adults to have the clearest, unmarked coats. A rich warm colour is necessary in kittens however, and there must be no sign of white on the throat or under the body, for a warm colour will never develop in a cold-toned coat, neither will white spotting miraculously disappear. The Abyssinian is not the easiest of cats to breed, the queen is sometimes slow in coming into oestrus, which then only lasts for a few days, during which time she may not 'call' lustily like other Foreign queens in season, but instead give soft chirruping cries. She may also have the rather shy and retiring nature typical of the breed, and so, when transported to the chosen stud cat, decide against cooperation. When she does breed successfully, the Abyssinian queen has an average of four kittens and, strangely, the greater proportion born are males. Most Abyssinian queens are very good mothers, keeping their litters clean and well-fed until weaning time.

The origins of the Abyssinian cats are rather obscure, although it is known that a queen called Zula was brought to Britain from Abyssinia (now called Ethiopia) in 1868, and that she closely resembled today's cats of the same breed. For a while they were called 'British Ticks', and then in 1929, with the formation of a breed club in Britain and a properly formulated standard, the breed was developed in earnest, and excellent foundation stock was sent to the United States in 1931.

Haj's Dynesty Tut is an American-bred silver Egyptian Mau, descended from cats brought originally from Cairo.

A natural breed developed to show standard in the United States is the EGYPTIAN MAU, which is similar in structure to the Abyssinian but has a coat which is distinctly spotted, instead of ticked. Spotted cats abound in Far Eastern countries, and like the Abyssinian cat are thought to have descended from *Felis libyca ocreata*, a spotted wild species. The first Egyptian Mau cats were brought from Italy to the United States in 1956, and their owner decided to develop the breed for exhibition purposes, finally gaining acceptance by the Cat Fanciers' Association in 1977. The Egyptian Mau cat is shy but very loving, again resembling the Abyssinian. It is an active cat and is said to learn tricks and to like riding around on its owner's shoulders. Similar in build to an Oriental Shorthair, the body is a little more cobby, and the head type is a modified wedge-brow, cheeks and profile all showing gentle curves, rather than the angular planes of the Siamese-derived varieties. The eyes are large and almond-shaped, slightly uptilted at the corners, and of a clear, light definite green shade.

All Mau must conform to the official pattern, which calls for a good contrast between the pale ground colour and the deeper markings. The forehead should carry the distinctive 'M', and frown marks and dark lines which continue over the top of the head and down to the back of the neck where they break up into elongated dots. The spine lines consist of dotted lines, which, as they reach the tail, form a dorsal stripe extending to its tip. Heavy rings band the tail and the body is heavily marked with random spots of variable size and shape. The markings may be dark brown on light bronze – the Bronze Mau; black on silver – the Silver Mau; or charcoal grey on silver – the Smoke Mau.

A universally popular breed is the BURMESE whose origins trace back to a brown cat called Wong Mau transported from Burma to the United States in 1930. Such self-brown cats were known to have existed in the Asiatic countries for many years, along with the Himalayan-patterned Siamese and the self-blue Korat. Wong Mau was mated with a Siamese male as there were no other Burmese available, and she had the curious kittens we now call TONKINESE. These 'hybrids', mated together, finally produced Burmese, Siamese and further Tonkinese offspring, and, over the years, the Burmese breed became established.

Cat Fanciers' Association recognition was granted in 1936 and some ten years later the first exciting imports were made into Britain. About this time, Cat Fanciers' Association withdrew registration privileges due to a dispute over breeding practices, and did not reinstate the breed until 1957. In the meantime, the Burmese had gained a good toe-hold in Britain, where the Governing Council of the Cat Fancy gave them official breed status in 1952, having been satisfied by records of three generations of breeding that the Burmese was a pure breed.

Burmese cats are strong and muscular and very active. They can be very mischievous, and if allowed to get out of hand, they can become destructive in the home. A properly brought-up Burmese is a delightful pet, intelligent and extremely affectionate. It is a breed that must not be left alone for long periods, or it will become morose and moody and may undertake some displacement activities. Pet Burmese do best in pairs, and romp their way through life, playing together right into old age. The short, close coat is very easy to groom with a silk cloth, and its active habits keep its body in good hard physical condition.

Burmese cats breed well and are very prolific. They mature early and the queens 'call' regularly and mate without too much fuss. Fairly large litters seem to be the norm in this breed, and the kittens are of a good size at birth, open their eyes during the first few days of life and progress by leaps and bounds. The kittens are generally precocious, trying out their dam's food at three to four weeks of age and growling over chunks of meat two weeks later. Born quite pale in colour, the true coat colour develops slowly and the kittens may well show ghostly tabby markings on the flanks and legs. Burmese are very contemporary cats fitting in well with present-day home life.

In the United States, the Cat Fanciers' Association recognizes only the Brown Burmese, which it calls Sable. In Britain the breed has been

This pair of Burmese kittens, looking uncharacteristically apprehensive, consists of a Blue on the left and a Brown, or Sable Burmese on the right.

The Lilac or Platinum Burmese is an attractive, pale cat with slightly darker colour on the points. Like all Burmese, the eyes should be of a golden yellow tone.

The Burmese are found in four tortoiseshell varieties, all of which are always female. This small kitten (right) is a Lilac-Cream or Lilac-Tortie.

This Cream Burmese has a strong head which fits the G.C.C.F. standard of points. The beautiful coat is clear of markings, but the eyes should not be so clearly green.

developed to its logical conclusion. Some of the original Brown cats occasionally produced Blue and Chocolate kittens, and when cats carrying both blue and chocolate genes intermated, Lilac Burmese kittens were born. As is usual, British breeders were not even satisfied with that range of Burmese colours, and so decided to add the sexlinked red-factor to the breed. Judicious outcrosses were made and the Red Burmese was born, along with Tortie females. With the addition of dilution genes, a Cream Burmese was produced, and a range of dilute Tortie females to be known as Blue-Tortie, Chocolate-Tortie and Lilac-Tortie depending upon the main shade displayed in the coat. The Torties are very beautiful indeed, and often display two shades of each of their two basic colours which may be either intermingled or patched. Tortie Burmese may have solid colour on their legs, paws and tails, and they may have blazes. Type is considered much more important than coat colour distribution in this breed, and no two Torties are ever alike, making them ideal pets for owners who want a totally unique cat.

The Burmese type in the United States differs from that in Britain, for although the cats came from the same root stock, differences in breeders' methods of selection have, over the years, created two quite different races. The American Burmese is a chunky cat, surprisingly heavy for its size, due to its strong bone and hard muscle development. It has a somewhat rounded head without any flat planes whether looked at from the front or in profile. There is good width between the eyes, which are slightly rounded and of any yellow shade, although brilliant gold is preferred. The nose is short with a distinct stop in profile.

The body of the Burmese should present a well-balanced but tough appearance, with well-proportioned legs and a slim, straight tail. The Burmese type in Britain is much finer, and while any tendency to Siamese-type conformation is considered a serious fault, so too is any suggestion of cobbiness or coarseness. The head should be a short, blunt wedge and the eyes must be neither round nor Oriental. Green eyecolour is considered to be a serious fault in the Brown Burmese but is not so severely penalized in the Blue variety. The Brown or Sable Burmese is a rich seal-brown, very slightly lighter underneath the body and very slightly darker on the ears and mask. Although genetically black, this variety should never appear black. The Blue variety is a soft silvery grey, fractionally darker on the back and tail. Chocolate Burmese are a very warm light brown and often have a slightly darker mask and ears, while the Lilac Burmese is a light dove-grey, with a warm pinkish cast. Red Burmese are light tangerine in colour and sometimes have very slight tabby markings, and the Cream Burmese may also have tiny markings on its rich cream coat.

Cheronia Red Oliver, a delightful Red Burmese male, wears his collar complete with identity tag.

Burmese are powerfully-built cats despite their modified Foreign type, and often feel surprisingly heavy and muscular for their size.

There are two breeds of blue Foreign Shorthairs recognized in both Britain and the United States, namely the KORAT and the RUSSIAN BLUE. Rare even in its native Thailand, the Korat is considered by the Thai people to ensure good luck if kept as a housepet. Known as the Si-Sawat in its country of origin, the cat is said to have been named by King Chulalongkorn when he commented upon the beauty of one of the silver-blue felines and was told that it came from the Province of Korat. Si-Sawat is a compound word in the Thai language and means a mingled colour of grey and light green. A pair of Korat cats are said to be a traditional gift for a Thai bride, and symbolize silver, to bring prosperity and happiness in the marriage. The Thai rain-making ceremony also requires the help of a Korat, referred to as the cloud-coloured cat with eyes of the colour of young rice.

All Korat cats can trace their ancestry back to original Thai stock, and its breed club, the Korat Cat Fanciers' Association, is dedicated to the protection of its pure breeding. Cats are sold complete with papers which include a contract signed by both seller and purchaser binding both to specific rules of conduct in all Korat cat matters. The Korat has a charming disposition and loves to be loved. It is a sociable cat and seems to prefer to live in small social groups than in grand isolation. The pet Korat soon builds up a rapport with its owner and likes to show its affection to people and other cats by its expressive gaze, sonorous purr and dainty tail-waving gestures.

Heart-shaped, the head of the Korat has considerable breadth between the eyes, which are large and luminous, and seem rather oversized for the face. Though rounded when open, the closed eyes show a decidedly Oriental slant and the colour preferred is a luminous green. Kittens and adolescents may have yellow or amber eyes as the true colour may take up to two or three years to develop fully. The Korat has large ears with rounded tips, flared at the base and set rather high on the head, giving the typically alert look of the breed. The body is strong and muscular with a curved back, and the tail is heavy at the base tapering to a rounded tip. The limbs should be in good balance with the body, the hind legs slightly longer than the forelegs, and the paws should be oval. The single coat of short, fine glossy hair is silver-blue all over, each hair having a distinctive silver tip.

Taking the sun in a London garden, a charming Russian queen, *Paramenta Astafaeva*.

Grand Champion Senty-Twix Jasper is a fine example of the Cornish Rex breed.

RUSSIAN BLUE cats were already well-known in Britain at the turn of the last century, and were said to have come from the port of Archangel in Northwest Russia, having travelled by merchant ship and been traded for goods by the seamen. When first exhibited in Britain in 1880, the breed immediately caught the interest of cat fanciers and general public alike, even though they were judged in the same class as the British Blue cats of that time. By 1912 the breed's name was changed to Blue Foreign in official circles, although the breeders continued to call their cats 'Russians', and eventually the name Russian Blue regained Cat Fancy approval. The most striking feature of this breed is the unique coat which should be short, thick and very fine, standing away from the skin, feeling soft and resilient to the touch. The coat colour is clear, even and distinct blue, medium tones are preferred in Britain and lighter shades in the United States. Bone structure is long and slender and the paws, small and oval. The long body is well balanced by an equally long, tapered tail. The standards for the head of the Russian differ considerably on either side of the Atlantic. In Britain the head should be short and wedge-shaped, the flat forehead forming an angle with the nose when viewed in profile, the whisker pads should be prominent, and the chin firm and strong. Large pointed ears, with wide bases, should be set vertically on the head. The eyes should be wide set, almond in shape and of a clear, vivid green tone.

Conversely, the Cat Fanciers' Association standard calls for a broad face with rounded eyes set wide apart, large, pointed and wide-based ears set far apart, as much on the side as on the top of the head. Russian Blue cats make undemanding pets. They are very hardy and need little attention, although they do seem to thrive on intelligent conversation with their owners, preferring family friends to strangers. They are gentle, quiet-voiced cats, affectionate and demure.

56

It was in 1950 that one of the kittens born to a farm cat in Cornwall, England, was seen to have a distinctly curled coat. He was retained and when adult, mated back to his mother, a Tortie-and-White domestic shorthaired cat. Several more curled kittens were born and eventually, with the help of experienced cat breeders, judicious outcrosses were made to strengthen the breeding lines. Crossing the curled cats with ordinary shorthaired varieties produced only straight-coated kittens, but when these were mated back together, a proportion of curled kittens were born; but if two curled cats were crossed, all their kittens were curled. Similar to Rex rabbit fur, the breed was called the CORNISH REX.

Ten years after the discovery of Kallibunker, the first Cornish Rex, another curly cat was found, this time in the neighbouring English county of Devon. Having seen the newspaper pictures of the Cornish Rex, called Poodle-cats and Coodles by journalists, a Devonshire lady realized that her own cat's litter containing a curly-coated male, might be of interest. She contacted the breeders of the Cornish cats and told them about Kirlee, her unusual pet.

Rex cat enthusiasts were very excited about the possibility of a new bloodline, and lost no time in making arrangements for a mating to take place between Kirlee and one of Kallibunker's descendants, and when Kirlee matured, this took place. All the kittens in the litter were straight-coated, thus proving that the Cornish curls and the Devon curls were caused by two quite separate and distinct genes. The long process of breeding programmes had to begin all over again with the second Rex strain, and several of Kirlee's straight-coated daughters were mated back to him. About half of their progeny were rexed and so the new breed was on the road to recognition. Both the CORNISH and the DEVON REX were officially accepted by the Governing Council of the Cat Fancy in 1967, and have made great progress since that time.

The Cornish is a cat of foreign type. Its medium wedge head is about one-third longer than its maximum width. The skull is flat and the face narrows to a firm chin. In profile, a straight line is seen from the centre of the forehead to the end of the nose. The fairly bold, oval eyes may be of any colour in keeping with that of the coat. All coat colours are acceptable. The ears are large and set quite high, giving a very alert look. The coat is short and plushy, and covers the body with deeply rippled waves. In body type, the Devon Rex is similar, but its head is shorter with full cheeks and the shortish nose has a distinct muzzle break. Huge ears, set rather low, and often sporting furry earmuffs, add to the clown-like look of this delightful breed, and once gave rise to its descriptive nickname the 'Butterfly Rex'. The coat of the Devon Rex is fine and softly curled, with soft down on the underparts, and even the whiskers and eyebrows are crinkled.

Devon Rex cats are great clowns and give their owners endless hours of entertainment. A favourite game is hide-and-seek.

Left: *Blue Betty Boop* likes to get a different slant on the world in general, alternating her real view with its mirrored image.

Right: Young Devon Rex kittens are often short of coat, especially under the body, and they have very short and crinkled whiskers too.

Right: A silver
Egyptian Mau
demonstrates his
balancing act.

Below: A pet Mi-Ke
cat from Japan,
tailless and aloof.

Two established breeds of cat were crossed to produce a new one, the strikingly handsome BOMBAY. The first cross was made between a black American Shorthair and a female Sable Burmese. Both parents were American Grand Champions, and the offspring appeared to combine their finest qualities. The Bombay breeds true, and so it was relatively easy to perpetuate the breed once the black colour was introduced. It is a happy cat with a good temperament and is very affectionate, especially to its owner. The head should be round, without flat planes and the face full with good width between the eyes. The muzzle is very strong and there should be a distinct nose-break. The beauty of this cat lies in the quality and appearance of its coat which is the shiny black of patent leather, short and close-lying, and very light-reflective, due to its satiny texture. Shining from the jet black face the large round eyes may be of any golden shade, though the deeper tones are favoured.

From a man-made breed, we now turn to a completely natural one which originated in Japan, and has been depicted, in paintings, carvings and murals, statues, woodcuts and on porcelain for many centuries. This is the JAPANESE BOBTAIL, which in its tri-coloured pattern is known as the Mi-Ke. The unique feature of this cat is, of course, its strange tail, which is carried upright and is only about 4 inches (10 cm) long. The tail may be straight or have one or more angles or curves. The cat's overall type is long and lean, with a well-muscled body and fairly long legs. The head is triangular with gentle lines and very high cheekbones, giving it a truly Japanese look, and the unusually set large ears add to this effect. Large oval eyes may be of any colour to harmonize with that of the coat. The coat is soft and silky, medium in length, and without a noticeable undercoat, while the hair on the tail is longer and thicker producing a pom-pom effect which disguises the underlying bone structure of the bobtail. Although all coat patterns except Siamese-Pointed or Abyssinian-type ticking are allowed, preference is given to dramatic markings and vivid colours.

The Bombay shines just like patent leather. This is *Gotagato T. Texas Tyler*, a Bombay male.

Oriental
and Siamese Cats

The original SIAMESE cats to arrive in Britain were a present from the King of Siam and given to the British Consul General in 1884. Such cats were very rare at that time, and the gift was deemed a great honour. A year later, a Seal Pointed Siamese was exhibited at the Crystal Palace Cat Show and the general public was enthralled by its unusual colouring and bold sapphire eyes. Pictures of those early Siamese show that they had round heads and were much heavier in build than today's exhibition Siamese. Some had twisted, knotted or kinked tails, and squinting eyes were quite common. They did have really pale coat colour however, in startling contrast to their points, and this is one characteristic of the old-type cats that present day breeders would love to regain. Some of the Siamese imported early this century proved to be very frail and many

The Siamese-derived Oriental cats have loving personalities and very beguiling ways. The kittens are very forward and adventurous. As they grow up, they quickly learn acceptable house manners and respond to words of praise. As adults, like *Chawalet Shimmering Lace*, the Foreign White (far right), they develop their final elegant and refined form.

died. They had no resistance to the usual low-grade infections, and animal husbandry also left a lot to be desired – some of the Siamese were kept in hot-house conditions, and fed on bread soaked in milk. Eventually it was realized that lots of fresh air and exercise, plus plenty of good fresh meat and drinking water would keep the Siamese in fine, healthy condition, and from that time onward, the breed began to flourish.

From the original Seal Point Siamese, natural recessive colours emerged quite naturally, and once these were accepted, were developed as separate varieties. The second colour to be officially recognized as Siamese was the Blue Point and a few years later the Chocolate Point joined the list. Later Siamese carrying both blue and chocolate genes were intermated and then the ethereal Lilac Point appeared. The Tabby Point group and the Red Point series are the results of cross-breeding, necessary to introduce the tabby and red factors respectively. Careful mating programmes were drawn up once the possibility of breeding these rare Siamese had been explored, and judicious first crosses were made, with the offspring being mated back to the very best available Siamese to regain type. As each colour variety reached the desired standard of perfection, the Governing Council of the Cat Fancy in Britain granted recognition.

Far right: *Solitaire Mulberry*, a Lilac Foreign and (top) *Solitaire Mallow*, her Lilac-Pointed litter sister. An adult Lilac-Pointed Siamese (above centre) and Silver Egyptian Mau kittens (below).

Siamese cats must conform to the same general standard, whatever the colour of their points, and the term 'points' refers to the mask or face, the ears, legs and paws, and the tail. The Himalayan genetic factor which causes the Siamese to be coloured only on its points, ensures also that such cats have blue eyes, regardless of the points colour. The Siamese is long, svelte and elegant, with graceful limbs and small oval paws. The long, wedge-shaped head has its lines accentuated by large, wide-based ears and the sapphire eyes are Oriental in shape slanting towards the nose. The profile should be straight, the chin strong and firm, and the teeth should meet in an even bite. From the head a long neck joins the slender body, and the tail should be equally long, tapering to a fine point. The coat is very short and fine textured, close-lying and with a healthy sheen.

Seal, Blue, Chocolate and Lilac Pointed Siamese are accepted as such on both sides of the Atlantic. However the Cat Fanciers' Association of the United States does not recognize the Tabby, Red and Tortie Pointed groups as Siamese but rather as COLORPOINT SHORTHAIRS. The Association has also changed the description, and calls the Tabby Pointed cats, 'Lynx Points'. The standards for the Siamese of Britain and the Siamese and Colorpoint Shorthairs of the United States are, however, virtually identical, and the different varieties are only distinguishable by the colour of their points. The Seal Point is a genetically black cat but its points' colour is affected in a very small way by the Himalayan factor, causing the black areas to look dark seal brown, and the body is fawn, shading to a darker tone on the back and the flanks. In the Blue Point, the body is of a cold tone shading to grey and the points are a deep slate-blue. Chocolate Point Siamese have ivory body colouring and their points are a rich milk-chocolate shade. The Lilac Point has a white body with points of a delicate pink-toned grey. Red Point Siamese or Colorpoints are very striking, with white bodies and dark orange points, while Cream Points are also stark white on their bodies with points of palest apricot.

The all-female Tortie Point Siamese come in four shades and each has the typically unique markings of the tortoiseshell, restricted to the areas of the points. The Seal Point has a cream to fawn body, and mottled points of dark brown, red and cream. Blue-Tortie Points or Blue-Cream Points have bluish-white bodies, while their points are mottled cream on blue-grey. In the Chocolate-Tortie or Chocolate-Cream Point, the body colour is ivory with warm milk-chocolate points mottled with cream. Lilac-Tortie, or Lilac-Cream Points have glacial white body colour and the points are very pale frosty grey mottled with very light cream. A Tortie Point may show a facial blaze.

The lilac colouring is modified by the addition of other genes. In the Lilac Oriental Tabby (right) a pink tone appears, while in the Lilac-Tortie Pointed Siamese (below) the colours are soft and muted.

Self Lilac kittens are evenly coloured from birth. *Solitaire Amarant* and *Amboyna* are six weeks old.

The Tabby Point Siamese, or Lynx Points, also come in a similar range of points colours, but instead of being mottled with red or cream, the typical markings are tabby. The Seal-Tabby has dark seal-brown patterning, the Blue-Tabby has slate-blue markings, the Chocolate-Tabby has warm milk-chocolate-striped points and the Lilac-Tabby has its pattern in pale, pinkish-grey. The tabby pattern on all of these varieties must conform to certain rules – for example, the colour should be fairly constant and the paws should not be many shades paler than the mask. Most judges bring the tail tip around to the cat's ears, and this not only helps to check whether the tail is a good length, it also tests whether or not the points match up correctly. The ears should be clearly coloured without any stripes, and each should have a clear central mark as though printed with a thumb. On the mask, the stripes should be very clearly defined, especially around the nose and eyes, and long pencilled lines should run from the cheekbones down to the neck. The whisker pads have distinct spots. The legs should have clear broken stripes of varying sizes, and the tail should be ringed and with a solid-coloured tip. In the rare Tortie-Tabby Pointed cats, both tortoiseshell and tabby patterns are clearly apparent, and this variety can also be bred in the standard range of points colours.

SIAMESE-DERIVED FOREIGN AND ORIENTAL SHORTHAIRS are just as their name suggests: man-made varieties developed from the basic Siamese Cat. By breeding-out the Himalayan factor which restricts the coat colour to the points of the Siamese cat, other cats of exactly the same bone structure and general characteristics were produced, but these had the coloration all over their bodies. In the Self-Coloured range we find the FOREIGN BLACK or EBONY, a jet black cat built like a miniature panther and with glowing green eyes; the self-coloured chocolate cat is known as the HAVANA in Britain and as the ORIENTAL CHESTNUT in the United States; and there is the FOREIGN LILAC or ORIENTAL LAVENDER, which is the solid-coloured version of the Lilac Pointed Siamese. Self-blue cats are also produced from time to time, but as the Korat and Russians are so well established there is little call for another Foreign Blue variety.

The FOREIGN WHITE is a superb example of planned breeding, for it is merely a Siamese cat disguised beneath a pure white overcoat. The breeding programmes began in earnest in 1962, when the dominant white factor was introduced to the very best strains of Siamese, and great care and attention were paid to scoring the stock so as to achieve the best type, as well as retaining all the most desirable characteristics of the Siamese. At first problems were encountered, such as an incidence of deafness in one strain, and some degree of head smudging in another. Variable eyecolour and a tendency to an unacceptable hair length were other snags, but with patient perseverance, these were overcome, and the Foreign White of today is an established breed in its own right, regularly taking top honours on the show benches of the world, outstanding in type and temperament.

Non-Self Siamese derived varieties have also been developed as quite separate breed groups, by the addition of the various tabby patterns, and the introduction of silver genes, as well as using the red factor. Many unusual-looking kittens have appeared in litters from time to time, and those have been so attractive that breeding lines have been replanned. The ORIENTAL SPOTTED TABBY was the first of the Non-Self group of 'foreigners' to be recognized by the Governing Council of the Cat Fancy in Britain, and four colours only were allowed in the beginning, corresponding with the four basic Siamese colours of black, blue, chocolate and lilac. In the tabby, these are the colours of the markings only, and do not refer to the base coat which is always paler. When the silver gene was added, plans for producing the whole silver series were made, hoping to achieve the results as seen in Persians. Breeders plan to have Oriental Chinchillas and Shaded Silvers, as well as the Smoke variety that arose without any problems. Oriental Silver Spotted cats proved fairly easy to breed, although correct spotting was not always there in the early days. But when other feline colours were added to the silver group, problems arose in determining exactly the correct colour designation of the extraordinary kittens produced.

Arnica and Ala have a great deal of fun at Christmas.

The HAVANA is the self-coloured equivalent of the Chocolate Pointed Siamese and has the identical conformation of long and well-proportioned wedge head, large pricked ears set wide apart and a good firm chin. The Oriental eyes change from baby-blue to a clear green when the Havana kitten reaches three months of age, and any tendency to yellow or copper tones in the iris is considered a serious fault in an adult. Medium in size with long, lithe lines, the Havana should be kept slim and trim with plenty of exercise. Its long legs should end in small and dainty oval paws, and the very long whip-shaped tail must not have any trace of the kink so often inherited from old Siamese lines. Most striking of all to those unfamiliar with the breed, is the rich dark brown of the glossy Havana coat, which, in the mature cat looks just like the shiny 'conkers' that fall from horse-chestnut trees in autumn. Very short and fine, the coat is close-lying and should be brown right down to the roots of each hair. Any tendency for ghostly tabby markings to show through the adult coat is faulted on the show bench, and the presence of white hairs in the coat is also incorrect. It was in the early 1950s that the first Havana cats were carefully planned and bred, although some self-brown kittens had occasionally turned up quite unexpectedly during other experimental cat matings.

Eventually, sufficient chocolate-coloured kittens were born to enable a pair to be sent to the United States, and from these and other breeding stock, a quite separate breed developed over the years, and is known as the HAVANA BROWN. This cat differs in several features from Britain's Havana, despite having the same root stock. Perhaps the most striking difference is in the head, for whereas the Havana has a totally Siamese head, that of the American Havana Brown has a puppy-dog look, being only slightly longer than its width. There is a distinct 'stop' at the eyes and the muzzle is pronounced and square. In 1958, having completed the requirements of the Governing Council of the Cat Fancy as regards breeding the required number of generations, breeders of the Havana cats applied for and were granted recognition. Unfortunately, it was thought by the executive committee that the name 'Havana' was too similar to that of a rabbit breed, produced for fur, and so the name 'Chestnut Brown Foreign Shorthair' was designated. This was used until 1970 when the Council agreed to change it to Havana.

Havana cats are the self-coloured equivalent of Chocolate-Pointed Siamese. They are loving, intelligent and make perfect pets. These examples from the author's *Solitaire Cattery*, are: (left to right) *Maoli, Moaniani, Champion and Premier Maneki Neko, Solo, Arnica* and *Ala*.

It was about this time that a whole new wave of enthusiastic fanciers decided to try to improve the general type, colour and eyecolour of the Havana, by literally starting again from the beginning, and using the very best available stock in their programmes. During the 1970s the breed enjoyed a great revival and started regularly winning Best in Show awards. The breeders also had a bonus, for some of the Siamese used for improving the strains were Lilac Pointed, and along with the Havana kittens, lovely lilac littermates were born. The FOREIGN LILAC is exactly the same as the Havana, except for the coat colour which is a delicate grey with a pinkish tone, neither too blue nor too fawn. Cats of this colour had been bred previously, but no serious attempt had been made to perfect them into an acceptable breed. The Lilacs of the 1970s were very beautiful, combining style, grace and elegance with their unusual colouring. They soon caught the imagination of the Cat Fancy, breeders, judges and pet owners alike. This new variety quickly completed the necessary breeding programmes required before applying for official acceptance, and although breeders wanted to call the breed Foreign Lavender, recognition was granted for Foreign Lilac.

Both Havana and Foreign Lilac Cats, known as ORIENTAL CHESTNUT and ORIENTAL LAVENDER by the Cat Fanciers' Association in America, are really delightful to keep. They have all the best traits of their Siamese ancestors, but none of the less attractive. For example, they have soft expressive voices and never yowl. Intelligent, and possessing calm, self-assured characters, they make ideal pets for families who like to take their pets with them in the car and on holidays. They show well and are particularly renowned for their composure while being judged. Obviously, the home environment and methods of rearing kittens do play a part in the character-building of cats, but in selecting the original breeding stock for these varieties, great store was set on choosing cats with good breeding records, good type, steady temperament and disease resistance. This care taken in the early days has ensured that the Havana and Foreign Lilac of today are almost perfectly behaved, beautiful to behold, strong and healthy. Very easy to keep in tiptop condition with the minimum of effort, the Foreign and Oriental Shorthairs need only a good high-protein diet combined with lots of exercise, and a firm hand-grooming daily.

The most ancient cats recorded historically are those which were
worshipped by the Egyptians of the nineteenth dynasty. The Papyrus of
Hunefer, in the Egyptian *Book of the Dead*, shows Ra the God of the Sun,
having taken the form of a spotted cat, killing the God of Darkness, the
serpent Apep. Other pictures made in Ancient Egyptian times also show
distinctly spotted and mackerel tabby cats, and the many bronze statues
and amulets depicted cats of elongated Oriental structure. In the 1960s, it
was decided to try to re-create the cat of Ancient Egypt, and the first
careful crosses were made in a British cattery between Tabby-Pointed
Siamese and Havana cats. The aim was to breed a cat of extreme Oriental
type, very long in the neck, and with the pronounced shoulder formation
of the cats in the bronze statuettes. A coat colour of rich chocolate
spotting on a light, bright cinnamon ground was the aim, and it was
hoped to develop the natural 'M' mark found between the ears of many
tabby cats, into a definite design resembling the sacred scarab beetle of
the Pharaohs.

Breeding cats of the correct type and a single colour is comparatively
simple, but the addition of a very decided and intricate pattern is more
difficult. It was only after years of dedicated care and quite ruthless
selection of stock that the ORIENTAL SPOTTED TABBY was bred to
recognition standard and accepted as a breed in 1979. Its fans and
followers had always called their breed the EGYPTIAN MAU, for this had
been the aim of their years of selective breeding, but the Governing
Council of the Cat Fancy in Britain rejected that evocative name in favour
of the more descriptive one chosen by their executive committee. Oriental
Spotted Tabby cats are bred in colours other than the original bronze
effect which is caused by the combination of agouti and chocolate genes.
The lilac variety is very beautiful, and the sable with black spotting is a
striking cat. Now silver spotted Orientals are being bred, with clear black
markings, giving a most exotic effect. All other tabby patterns are being
developed by the members of the Oriental Tabby Cat Club in Britain, but
they are concentrating on producing the first perfectly spotted Champion
of good type, as well as developing classic marbled Oriental tabbies, in
shades of sable, silver and bronze.

Pet Cats

Small kittens are happy when they have a warm, safe bed in which to sleep.

Baskets also make good hiding places for kittens from which they can suddenly leap out.

Young kittens of any type have very appealing ways.

Every cat has a degree of dignity and retains the independent spirit of its past ancestry and its wild relatives. Whether it has a full pedigree dating back over a century of pure breeding, or whether it is the product of years of chance matings makes not an iota of difference – the domestic cat is essentially a pet animal and should be treated as such. House cats come in every conceivable colour, shape and size, and while the majority are shorthaired, some very pretty longhaired cats are seen from time to time. In Britain, non-pedigree cats may be affectionately referred to as 'Moggies' while in the United States they are distinguished from their pedigreed cousins by being called 'Domestics'. It is interesting to note that cats which make their own matrimonial arrangements might have stronger, healthier kittens; probably due to the fact that only the toughest free-ranging male cat in a neighbourhood manages to mate with the female cat in season. The Darwinian hypothesis of 'the survival of the fittest' is upheld by feral cat populations the world over.

Villages and small townships surrounded by large areas of countryside may well develop their own indigenous cat populations, due to the semi-isolation of the gene pools, and the coloration of the dominant tom-cats in these areas. The same effect is seen on some small islands, where very distinctive groups of cats develop, unaided by man. One region may have cats in which red predominates, and many of the local domestics are ginger, tortoiseshell or black-and-white, due to the random juggling of the genes. In other areas, blue cats might have taken over, the product of the diluting effect of the gene often called the Maltese factor, which reduces the pigmentation of black coat colour in many animals, to an attractive grey-blue. In some areas, the influence of the gene for Siamese patterning may be apparent, and was possibly introduced years before when a Siamese male cat had been allowed a degree of freedom. In combination with many other genes, these cats can be most unusual and often have tabby points with piebald spotting, which gives them blue eyes, and long white stocks, white bibs and possibly a blaze.

The character of a cat is controlled to a large extent by the things learned as a kitten in the impressionable days from its first steps out of the nest, until it is weaned. It has to absorb an enormous amount of information during that short period, information essential for its survival if it lived in a wild situation. At this stage, some massive development of the brain takes place and so its environmental conditions, experiences and diet all have important effects on the young cat. Some cats, born as feral kittens, may be tamed later, but will never be as docile and even-tempered as kittens born and raised in the normal, noisy, loving home. Wild or farm kittens need to be taken from their mothers at about six weeks of age and given extra handling and tender loving care to imprint them with some desirable habits. If they are caught and tamed later than twelve weeks of age, many traits will have been fixed and will prove difficult, if not impossible to change. Some pedigree cats also show some nervous and seemingly irrational behaviour patterns, and it can be interesting to trace their past history. It may be discovered that they were not handled regularly, or subjected to sufficient forms of stimuli during that important and sensitive period in their kittenhood.

Kittens need lots of toys and games to stimulate the development of their reflexes.

When choosing a new kitten, the same criteria apply whether it is a pedigree or non-pedigree. It is best to see the whole litter if possible, with their mother, and to take notice of things such as the healthy appearance of the cats and their general behaviour. The kittens should be playful and alert. Their eyes should be bright, with no sign of any weeping or discharge at the inner corners, and the inside of the ears should be clean and moist. Dark grits here can indicate infestation with ear-mites which gives rise to an irritating condition often called canker. Each kitten should have a dry nose and the coat should be soft and free from any little black specks excreted by cat fleas. The fur at the tail end should also be soft and clean, without any sign of staining which could point to the kitten having diarrhoea.

The mother cat may not look her best. She might well be very thin, having expended all her own bodily reserves in producing the large quantities of milk taken by her rapidly-growing litter, but her eyes should be bright and she should look happy and contented.

It is often very difficult to choose a kitten, and whenever possible it is best to have two from the same litter. Cats, contrary to popular belief, do not like to be left alone, and as some cats are confined to the house for long hours without human company, they may enjoy the association of another cat, especially if the two have been raised together. A kitten should be at least eight weeks old before it is taken to a new home, and in the case of Foreign and Oriental varieties, it should be at least twelve weeks. At three months of age the kitten should have had a vaccination against Feline Infectious Enteritis.

74

Introducing the kitten to its new home should be carried out calmly and quietly, for the little creature will be very stressed with the change in its environment. Let him explore and familiarize himself with just one room at first, and make sure that there are no hazards around, such as an unguarded fire or exposed heater, live electric flex to chew with needlesharp teeth, surfaces to fall from, or tiny spaces into which he can creep and hide. Give him a warm, private bed and offer some of his favourite food, putting fresh water in a shallow bowl, in an accessible spot. Lots of love and petting will assure the kitten of your very best intentions, and he will quickly transfer the affection he had for his mother over to you. Provide a shallow tray with a layer of the cat-litter that he knows. The first night in a new home can be very traumatic for the little kitten and he may cry for his family. A rubber bottle filled with hot water, and carefully wrapped, may be tucked in his bed to give some comfort, and a gently ticking clock placed by the bed is thought to calm the young kitten, providing a simulated heart-beat effect. After a very short while the kitten will have adjusted and will progress by leaps and bounds, if fed on the diet advised by his breeder, and kept warm, clean and amused.

Kittens find amusement in all manner of household objects, especially those that they can climb onto, into or through. Kittens particularly enjoy tucking themselves into small spaces from which they can peek out, ready to pounce. As they grow larger and stronger, they prefer to climb to high vantage points, jumping down to scare their littermates in mock hunting attacks.

If not already vaccinated, the kitten may receive injections against various diseases from three months of age. These vaccinations must be given by a veterinary surgeon, who will first examine the kitten to ensure that it is in good health. This is a very good time to discuss a programme of worming treatment and, if the kitten is not to be used for breeding purposes, the best age for neutering or spaying. Although veterinary surgeons each have their own preferences, most now seem to agree that the kittens should be well grown before neutering. Although they will perform the operations before, six to eight months seems to be the ideal age for both males and females. Some people like to allow a female cat to have a litter of kittens before she is spayed, but if this happens, the spaying operation is more serious than when it is performed on an adolescent kitten. The female cat matures at about nine months of age, and if kept for breeding, is called a 'queen'.

Pedigree male cats kept for breeding purposes are always provided with their own private and exclusive apartments in which they live, and receive visiting queens for service. Such cats, although confined to quarters to prevent fighting or catching infections from other cats, are treated like lords, loved and cherished by their owners, and fed on the very best of food. These males are often top award-winning cats having been shown extensively when young to build their reputations, in order to attract good quality mates. They are known as Stud Cats.

All cats, whether they have pedigrees or not, may be entered in cat shows. Pedigree cats must be registered with the official bodies, but any unregistered cat may enter the housepet sections arranged by many show committees. Cat magazines and periodicals give details of forthcoming feline-orientated events, with addresses of clubs, associations and show managers, from whom information and also help and advice may be obtained. By joining a cat club or society, it is possible to meet other people who make an enjoyable hobby out of exhibiting their cats.

Both pedigree and non-pedigree cats may enter most cat shows, where each exhibit is provided with a safe show pen. Below a magnificent Red Persian awaits the arrival of the judge.

These three-month-old pet kittens are just old enough to start competing. Here they enjoy the sunshine with their protective mother.

The show cat must be in excellent health, free from all parasites and with a well-groomed appearance. Top condition in cats is produced by feeding a well-balanced diet, containing the correct proportions of the nutrients required by the animal, and giving daily attention to the coat. Longhaired varieties need brushing and combing thoroughly every day, while the shorthaired varieties should be combed to remove dead hair, then buffed up with a pad of cloth, or the hands, in order to promote muscle tone. This in turn gives a healthy glow to the coat. All cats should have their ears checked and cleaned if necessary every week, and this is particularly important in the show cat. The claw beds too, should be kept clean and tidy, and there is an area along the top of the tail which sometimes gets greasy. If such a patch appears, it may be gently washed with soap and water, rinsed and dried, then combed back into place. Cats may be bathed if necessary, but this should be done at least five days before a show to enable the coat to settle down again. The coat may be cleaned and brightened by applying talcum or a proprietary brand of grooming powder. This is rubbed into the coat and given time to absorb any dirt or grease before being brushed thoroughly out again. No trace of powder must be left in the coat as this causes disqualification at the cat show. Quite strict rules and regulations are laid down for exhibitors at shows, and they must be read carefully and obeyed.

Showing provides a lot of fun and can be the perfect pastime for the pet owner as long as it is not taken too seriously. Cats are penned during exhibition and are not paraded on leashes like dogs at dog shows. Show cats should be accustomed to spending a few hours in a similar pen, at home, before being shown for the first time, or they may find the first outing a little unnerving. It is also essential to have a secure carrier in which to transport the cat. This may be of mesh, perspex, wood or wickerwork as long as it has a safe catch and is escape-proof. Many cats love shows, and become excited whenever they see the carrier.

Cats should be trained to enjoy going in their carriers, especially if they are to have a show career.

Healthy kittens
should have bright
shining eyes, soft
clean coats and be
alert and happy.

Kittens love to climb
and explore but must
be protected from all
sorts of hazards found
in the home.